Pouter Pigeon.

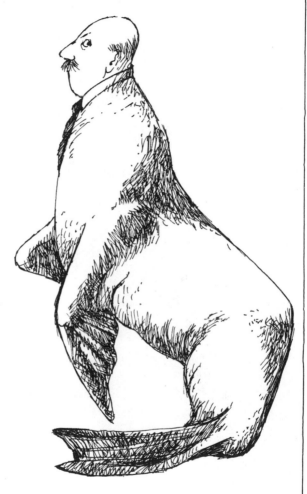

Sea Lion.

THE QUEEN'S NOSE

ALSO BY DICK KING-SMITH

Magnus Powermouse

ILLUSTRATED BY MARY RAYNER

The Queen's Nose

by

Dick King-Smith

Illustrated by Jill Bennett

Harper & Row, Publishers

The Queen's Nose
First published in Great Britain in 1983 by Victor Gollancz Ltd, London
Text copyright © 1983 by Dick King-Smith
Illustrations copyright © 1983 by Jill Bennett
Printed in
the United States of America. For information address
Harper & Row Junior Books, 10 East 53rd Street,
New York, N.Y. 10022.
Designed by Trish Parcell
10 9 8 7 6 5 4 3 2 1
First American Edition

Library of Congress Cataloging in Publication Data
King-Smith, Dick.
   The queen's nose.

   Summary: Ten-year-old Harmony, who loves animals but
isn't allowed to keep a pet, is given a magic coin with
seven wishes.
   1. Children's stories, English. [1. Wishes—Fiction.
2. Magic—Fiction] I. Bennett, Jill, ill. II. Title.
PZ7.K5893Qe 1985   [Fic]   83-49480
ISBN 0-06-023245-5
ISBN 0-06-023246-3 (lib. bdg.)

Contents

THE QUEEN'S NOSE

CHAPTER I

Uncle Ginger

Harmony and Rex Ruff Monty sat side by side in the old chicken house at the bottom of the garden.

No chickens had lived there for many years—Mr. and Mrs. Parker did not like animals—but a vague sour smell of the birds lingered on. There was still some musty straw in the nest boxes, and the perches were barnacled with old dry droppings.

The place was small and dark, for there was only one little wire-netting window, with a wooden shutter that you could slide shut if the rain blew in; the door was low, so that a grown-up person would have found it hard to enter; and, except for the perches, there was nothing to sit on but an upturned tea chest.

None of this mattered to Harmony, for the chicken house was her retreat. Here she came to be alone, which she mostly liked to be. Not of course that she was ever quite alone. There was always Rex Ruff Monty.

Harmony Parker was a girl of ten. She had very large brown eyes. She looked as though she wouldn't say "Boo!" to a goose. This was true in one sense, for she wouldn't have said anything so silly. A goose was one of the dozens of different creatures she dreamed

about owning as she sat on her tea chest. Harmony longed to have an animal of her own.

"I *wish* I could," she said to Rex Ruff Monty. "As well as you, I mean."

Rex Ruff Monty was a dog of fifty-nine. He had only one eye; the other had dropped out. He had first belonged to Harmony's grandmother and had originally been a rich chocolate color and quite hairy. Now he was gray and bald all over. He was recognizably some sort of large terrier, an Airedale perhaps. Three of his legs were still quite stiff, but the fourth, the right foreleg, was squidgy and elongated and even more hairless than the rest of him. It was by this leg that Harmony always carried him.

"Why do they have to be so mean?" she said. She picked up Rex Ruff Monty, who was standing on the tea chest awkwardly, tipped over on his soft leg with his blind side toward her, and turned him around.

"You tell me," she said, staring earnestly into his eye, "why they have to be so stupid about the whole thing. It isn't as though I wanted an elephant. Or half a dozen chimpanzees. Or a troupe of circus horses. I mean, I wouldn't mind all those but I'll settle for a pair of mice or just a gerbil. But they won't let me, and you know why, don't you?"

Harmony waited, for ten seconds perhaps, as you would when having a telephone conversation, and then continued.

"Exactly. You're absolutely right, Rex Ruff Monty. Mummy thinks animals are dirty and carry diseases."

There was another pause.

"Who? Oh, Daddy. Well, he's just not interested. Doesn't like animals. I'm not even sure he likes people much."

Pause.

"Except her of course, you're right, I forgot about Simple Sissie." Simple Sissie was Harmony's elder sister, Melody. She was fourteen and supposedly her father's favorite. She thought a great deal about her hair and her clothes. She referred to Rex Ruff Monty as "that filthy beast," and called his owner Harm.

"So what can I do?"

"Just keep on wishing, you say? Wishing will make it so, you say? Oh, Rex Ruff Monty, I *wish* it was as easy as that," and Harmony picked him up by his soft leg and undid the latch of the chicken house door.

She walked slowly up the orchard, swinging Rex Ruff Monty gently from side to side. There had been a summer shower and the long grass was wet. It felt pleasantly cool against her legs and on her bare feet, like paddling in the sea. Suddenly she dived behind an apple tree and lay flat, one hand pressed over the old dog's black woollen mouth, as her sister came out through the french windows and called her name.

"Harm!" cried Melody in her usual bossy voice. "Where are you? Mummy wants you."

Harmony burrowed lower.

"Not a sound, Rex Ruff Monty," she whispered. "Wait till you see the whites of her eyes."

She listened with pleasure to the repeated calling, and then to another voice, her mother's.

4

"Run down and fetch her, Melody darling. I know she's somewhere in the garden."

"Oh, Mummy, the grass is soaking! And I've got my new shoes on."

"Hurry up, darling."

"Oh, Mummy!"

Picking her feet up high, Melody moved reluctantly into the wet jungle of the orchard. In the depths of the jungle the tigress crouched, grinning with anticipation.

"Harm!" cried Melody once more. "Where are you? Oh, come on, you little beast!"

At this invitation the tigress charged.

Two very different sounds came to the ears of the three people who sat in the room behind the french windows.

The first was a kind of horrid, throaty, grunting, bubbling, coughing roar, not very deep in tone, to be sure, but of a ferocity that was heart stopping. And the second was a very loud scream.

"Oh, my nerves won't stand it!" cried Mrs. Parker, levering her plump self out of her armchair. "What on earth was that?"

Her husband placed the tips of his fingers together and looked carefully at them over his half-glasses.

"I fear," he said acidly, "that you have sent poor Melody into an ambush. Such a vivid imitation of the sound of a wild animal can only have been the work of your younger daughter." (Mr. Parker always re-

ferred to Harmony thus.) He looked over his finger-
tips at the man sitting opposite.

"I imagine," he said, "that you, Ginger, with your
encyclopedic knowledge of brute beasts, may actually
have recognized the sound?"

"Bengal tiger," said the other without hesitation.
"Heard one only last month, up at Bud Bud, just
before I came on leave. Didn't know there were any
in Wimbledon."

At this moment two figures burst in from the garden. One, the man called Ginger could see, was fair-
haired, with very large brown eyes and an expression
of angelic innocence. The other, larger and darker,
had obviously just taken a nasty tumble. Her rather

frilly summer dress was damp and rumpled and marked
with grass stains.

"Melody darling!" cried Mrs. Parker. "Whatever . . . ?"

The victim of the ambush was torn between burst-
ing into tears of rage and attacking her younger sister.
Disliking the first alternative as too babyish and dis-
missing the second as too dangerous (for Harmony
was a gutter fighter, no holds barred), she fled the
room, her mother in anxious attendance.

"Harmony," said Mr. Parker in a weary voice, "this
is my brother and therefore your uncle, home on leave
from India. I think he has never met you. At this
moment I can only consider him fortunate. Now, if
you will excuse me . . . ." He rose and moved heavily
out of the room.

"I'm Harmony," said Harmony. She put out a rather dirty hand. The man stood up and shook it with a very large one.

"My name's Henry," he said, "but everybody calls me Ginger." They looked at each other with interest.

One saw a small girl, bare legged, dressed in a pair of old jeans that had been hacked off at the knees and a faded T-shirt that advised him to "Save the Whale." Her feet were not clean, and she smelled faintly of chickens.

The other unhesitatingly saw an animal.

Long ago, Harmony had firmly decided that, with a few exceptions, animals were nicer than humans. People whom she knew or met she therefore saw in her mind, with the ease of long practice, as this or that mammal or bird or fish, even as an insect (her teacher was a female Praying Mantis).

She drew well, and expressed this fancy by portraits where the head of the person surmounted the body of the chosen animal. Locked away in her bedroom was a large scrapbook on the first page of which strutted a tubby fussy Pouter Pigeon bearing above its proud throat her mother's neat and rather vacant face. Overleaf, large, sleek and mustached, the eyes prominent beneath the bald crown, sat her father the Sea Lion. Opposite, Melody, her blue eyes only the merest fraction crossed, admired her Siamese reflection in a tall looking glass; not a hair was out of place on her glossy coat, and her long tail curled elegantly around her neat feet.

Sea Lion.

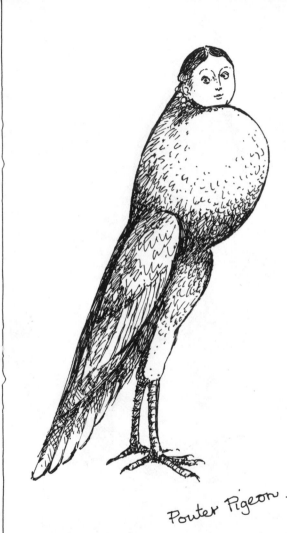

Pouter Pigeon.

Siamese Cat.

Now, looking at Uncle Ginger, bulky and tweedy, those large hands hanging loosely at the end of very long arms, Harmony instantly recognized a bear. And not just any bear. For though the color that had given him his nickname still held good in beard and mustache, the plentiful hair of his head was speckled with early gray. A Silvertip Grizzly!

They both spoke at once.

"You're not much like Daddy," said Harmony, and "You're not much like your sister," said the Silvertip, and they laughed comfortably together.

"Would you like to see the garden?" Harmony said. "I'll show you my den."

"Tiger's den?"

"Oh. You knew what I was pretending to be? Of course you would if you've spent a long time in India. Though there aren't many left, I believe."

"Not many."

"Have you ever seen one? In the jungle, I mean?"

"Yes, quite a few. And it was a very good imitation. How did you know the kind of noise an angry tiger makes?"

"Oh, films on T.V. And I've heard them at the zoo. Not angry, but hungry. And homesick, I expect."

"You don't like zoos?"

"I'm not sure. I know the good things about them. I just feel all animals ought to be happy and you can't be happy unless you're free."

They reached the chicken house. The Silvertip Grizzly

Silvertip Grizzly.

bent himself double to get through the door, was politely offered the tea chest, and sat down on it, head bowed under the low roof, long arms dangling. He looked at Harmony balanced on a perch.

"You're pretty keen on animals, are you?" he said.

"Yes. I like animals more than . . ."

"More than what?"

"More than most things."

"What have you got?"

"Animals, you mean?"

"Yes."

There was a pause.

"None," said Harmony.

Uncle Ginger raised his head rather sharply at this and hit it on the chicken house roof.

"No dog?" he said. "No cat? No rabbits, guinea pigs, mice, canaries, nothing?"

Harmony shook her head. She scuffed at the floor with a bare big toe, making large capital letters in the powdery mixture of old sawdust that covered it. Uncle Ginger, sitting opposite, read the word upside down. It said:

"That's what Mummy and Daddy think animals are," said Harmony in a flat voice. "The only way I'm ever going to own an animal, any animal, is by some sort of magic. D'you believe in magic, Uncle Ginger?"

"Yes. I do."

"They have lots of magic in India, don't they? Rope tricks and snake charmers and people lying on beds of nails and stuff?"

"Yes."

"D'you know anything about magic? Yourself?"

"A bit."

"Gosh! I *wish* you could use some of it while you're here. By the way, how long are you here for?"

"Couple of weeks."

They looked at each other.

"No," said Uncle Ginger, smiling through his beard, "I'm not just going to go to your parents and say, 'Harmony ought to have a puppy or a rabbit or something.' That's between you and them. But I might be able to help."

"Oh, I *wish* you would!"

They made their way out of the chicken house, and Uncle Ginger stretched himself. He looked up at the blue sky and then down at the brown eyes watching him. "D'you do a lot of wishing, Harmony?" he said.

"Yes," said Harmony. She pulled Rex Ruff Monty's raggedy ears.

From the top of the garden they heard voices calling.

"Ginger!" barked the Sea Lion. "There's a cup of tea ready."

And, "Harmony!" cooed the Pouter Pigeon. "Come and get tidy."

The Siamese Cat was sulking and made no sound.

"Wishes do come true, don't they?" said Harmony in a small voice. "Sometimes?"

The Silvertip Grizzly put a big paw on her shoulder and nodded his head.

"Sometimes," he said.

CHAPTER 2

Treasure Hunt

Those first two weeks of the summer holidays seemed to Harmony to go in a flash. She woke up one morning with the certain feeling that there was something nasty about that particular day. Of course! Uncle Ginger was going, first down to Devonshire to stay with some friends, and then back to India.

It was a lovely sunny morning, just the sort when usually Harmony would be up in a hurry and outside, leaving the Sea Lion and the Pouter Pigeon snoring their distinctive snores and the Siamese curled lazily in her neat bed. But this morning she lay still, Rex Ruff Monty by her side, and thought about everything that had happened. What a lot of treats they had had. Uncle Ginger had taken them to all sorts of things, sometimes the whole family but mostly just the two girls. Once he and she had gone alone, to the Natural History Museum, because Simple Sissie had said she had a headache; and Harmony had wondered if there would be any more talk about magic. "I might be able to help"—that's what the Silvertip had said. But there wasn't. And now he was going.

"And another thing," she said to Rex Ruff Monty. "He's bought everybody presents except me. Flowers

17

and chocolates for Mummy, cigars for Daddy, a dress for Simple Sissie. What d'you make of that?"

"Jealous, you say, I'm jealous? Oh, come on, Rex Ruff Monty, of course I'm not."

But she was.

Then the thought occurred to her, not just that she hadn't been given a present, but that she hadn't been given a present—yet!

She decided to give Rex Ruff Monty the credit.

"Of course, of course, how absolutely right you are as always. He's saving up my present till last, till just before he goes. Because it's something very special! Of course!"

Harmony suddenly felt ridiculously happy. She lay in bed a little longer, making faces for the benefit of her one-eyed audience. First she made a Jealous Face, pulling the corners of her mouth down, gritting her teeth, nostrils flaring, brow furrowed. Then she gradually changed this, through a Suddenly Realizing Face— eyebrows raised, eyes and mouth slowly opening wide—to a Ridiculously Happy Face, split right across in a huge grin.

Of course! It was something very special! But what? It couldn't be a pet of any kind—Uncle Ginger had said he wouldn't interfere in that—but it might be a book about animals perhaps. Or maybe model animals for her farm, which was spread all over her bedroom floor. A very mixed farm it was, for zebra and deer mingled with the cows, there were hippos among the pigs and ostriches amid the chickens, and on the shiny glass surface of the duck pond a crocodile bared his ever open jaws.

Or perhaps—surprisingly her mind moved for a moment away from birds and beasts—it would be a soccer ball; he knew she was keen on that. It couldn't be that pair of brilliant red-and-gold-striped soccer socks she'd always longed for; she hadn't told him about them.

Or possibly, just possibly, could it be a bike, a new bike!

Don't be so silly Harmony, she said to herself, and she put on her Don't Be So Silly Harmony Face (the sort you make on meeting a very nasty smell), and leaped out of bed. As usual, Rex Ruff Monty's face was expressionless.

After breakfast Mr. Parker left as usual for his office in the city. Watching the two brothers say their good-byes, Harmony thought how unlike they were, as

unlike indeed as you would expect a Sea Lion and a Silvertip Grizzly to be. One she would see again that evening, the other . . . goodness knows when. Perhaps never. Her heart suddenly felt as though someone had squeezed it.

I *wish* Uncle Ginger wasn't going, she said silently to Rex Ruff Monty lying upside down in her lap, I *wish*, I *wish*, I *wish*. Her lips must have moved, because the Silvertip grinned and said, "Wishing again, Harmony?"

Harmony felt herself go very red and was glad that the Pouter Pigeon had fluttered off to preen herself and the Siamese had slid away to stare into the nearest looking glass.

Ginger saw the blush and changed the subject.

"Oh, by the way," he said, "I've got a present for you. It isn't much but it might help. I'll go up and get it. Anyway I must collect my bags and make a start. I've got quite a long drive," and he went out of the room with his rolling grizzly's gait.

Harmony sat quite still. On both hands her fingers were crossed. Everyone likes getting presents, but more and more she had come to feel that this one was going to be very special.

"It isn't much," he had said, so it couldn't be a bike. A watch perhaps, a digital with a thick leather strap, not a silly little ornamental one like Simple Sissie's. Or it might be one of those pens that wrote in six different colors.

Uncle Ginger came downstairs again, a suitcase in

each hand, and loaded them into the car that he had hired for his leave.

He called, "Harmony!"

Harmony uncrossed her fingers and ran outside, Rex Ruff Monty swinging by his soft leg.

"Yes, Uncle Ginger?"

"This is for you. Now, I'll go and find your mother and Melody to say my good-byes and then I must be off."

Harmony looked at the small, thin brown envelope in her hand. Money, she thought, and a little wave of disappointment washed over her. She was not a greedy child and it did not occur to her that a small envelope can contain a valuable bank note. She just felt that money was an impersonal present, that she had wanted some *thing*, any thing however humble—never mind about watches or bikes—to remind her of the big man who now came out of the house with her mother and sister. But just money!

"Thank you very much," she said.

"What have you got, Harm?" cried Melody, and she twirled, catlike, to show off her new dress.

"Open it, Harmony darling," cooed her mother. "You can't thank Uncle Ginger when you don't know what you're thanking him for!"

"Oh, yes, she can," said Uncle Ginger quickly, and he winked at Harmony, a very small private wink that the others did not see.

"Anyway it is I who should be doing all the thanking, for putting me up and putting up with me. You've been very kind and I've thoroughly enjoyed my stay," and he enveloped the Pouter Pigeon and the Siamese in a bear hug.

Then he turned to Harmony but she only stuck out her hand. The Silvertip Grizzly took it gently in his large paw. He looked down from his great height at the brown eyes that seemed larger than ever, at the pale face that was set in a tight frozen smile.

"Good-bye, Harmony," he said. "Don't forget— good things come in small packages," and he climbed into the car and drove away, waving until the bend in the drive hid him from sight.

"What did he mean by that?" asked Mrs. Parker.

"I expect," purred Melody, "he was referring to your younger daughter's being such an extremely short person, not to say a dwarf."

Normally such a remark would have invited instant attack, or at the least Harmony's I Hate My Sister Face, eyes horribly crossed and tongue almost touching her chin; but to Melody's surprise she seemed not to have heard. She walked into the house and locked herself in the downstairs bathroom.

"Sulking. Silly child," mewed Melody.

Mrs. Parker pouted.

"I simply don't understand her," she said. "Did you notice, she wouldn't kiss your uncle. She seems to have no affection for people."

Sitting on the toilet seat, Harmony opened the brown envelope. Inside there was only a scrap of paper. On it was written in capital letters:

THEY GROW IT IN INDIA.

Harmony leaped off the seat.

"I ought to have known, Rex Ruff Monty!" she said in a fierce whisper. "Of course he wouldn't have just given me boring old money! It's the first clue in a treasure hunt!

"What's that you say? Wait till we're on our own? You're absolutely right, as usual."

She unlocked the door and went to find her mother.

"Are you going out this morning, Mummy?"

"Yes, darling, Melody and I are going shopping, in about half an hour. Why, d'you want to come?"

"No thanks. I haven't got any money."

"Oh, so it wasn't even money in the envelope then?"

said Melody cattily. "What was it then?"

"Mind your own stinking business."

"Harmony! Really! You are not to speak to your sister like that."

Harmony ran upstairs and, once safely out of sight, made her My Mother Drives Me Mad Face, sticking her thumbs in her ears and waggling her fingers, at the same time screwing her mouth sideways, tongue drooling over her lower lip like an idiot.

She waited impatiently till she heard the car drive away, and then dashed for the encyclopedias on the living room bookcase.

"Here we are, Rex Ruff Monty. Now then, I to M, where's India? Ah, here it is . . . 'climate mainly tropical monsoon; agric. economy (esp. rice, cotton, timber, tea).' Now, let's be methodical. Remember what the Praying Mantis is always saying—'Harmony Parker, you are slapdash. You must learn to be more methodical.' So, rice first."

In the kitchen the rice was in a large screw-top jar. She opened it and there seemed to be nothing in it but rice. She tipped out the contents onto a sheet of newspaper but nothing was hidden among the grains. There was a packet of rice unopened in the larder. She looked to see if anything was written on it, but no.

"Cotton then."

She went carefully through the drawers of her mother's sewing table. Cotton thread there was in plenty, but no clue. What else was made of cotton?

24

Sheets perhaps. She searched all the bedrooms. Blank.

"OK then, timber."

Well, all right, loads of things in the house were made of wood, but timber meant growing trees, didn't it? Doggedly she climbed in turn the three knobbly old apple trees in the orchard, Rex Ruff Monty lying patiently in the grass to leave both her hands free. But to no avail.

"It must be tea, then."

There were several tea containers in the house. There were two tins in the kitchen, one with Indian tea, one with China tea ("though that would be cheating if he put a clue there"). There was a handsome fluted caddy in the silver tea service her mother used on special occasions. There was a zinc-lined box shaped like a miniature sea chest, made of a pale polished wood and brass bound. All were full of tea and empty of information.

Automatically Harmony made her way to the place where she did her best thinking, the chicken house. She sat down and assumed her Concentrated Thought Face, which she always used at school when asked something she didn't know, eyes tight shut, head resting on hand, agonized expression. Rex Ruff Monty hung upside down from her other hand, and absently she swung him, thump, thump, thump against the tea chest on which she was sitting. Boom-ty, boom-ty, boom-ty said a bit of Harmony's busy brain as she thumped, and then boom-ty, boom-ty, boom-*tea*!

Of course! Quickly she jumped off the tea chest and tipped it over.

On the floor beneath it was another piece of paper. On it was written:

ALL THESE ARE WHAT ?
BETS, GHOSTS, PLANS,
FALSE TRAILS, FOUNDATION STONES.
SO ARE THESE.

Harmony did not know the word for placing a bet or exorcising a ghost and she would probably have said that you "make" a plan, but she knew the last two.

"False trails are 'laid,' " she said, "and so are foundation stones. What else? Of course! Eggs!"

Falling on her knees she searched feverishly in the dusty old straw of the four nest boxes. The first three had nothing in them. In the fourth her fingers touched something. Another envelope. On it was written:

HARMONY PARKER.

HANDLE WITH CARE.

This time there was something inside it, something small and hard. She tore the envelope open. Inside it there was a piece of paper. Hastily she unfolded it and out upon the powdery floor of the chicken house fell a single fifty pence piece.

CHAPTER 3

The Riddle

"Good things come in small packages." Was this all that he had meant? One fifty pence piece? Just money after all, nothing special. Harmony picked the coin up and put it in her pocket. She looked at the envelope again. "Handle with care."

Why? What could that mean? Then she noticed that there was writing on the piece of paper in which the money had been wrapped, and felt a sudden tingle of excitement. The hunt wasn't over then! More clues!

Carefully she smoothed it out and read it, first quickly to herself and then aloud and slowly for the benefit of Rex Ruff Monty:

YOU AND I DO SHARE A YEAR
YOU WILL WANT TO KEEP ME NEAR

SIX TIMES MORE WHEN ONCE YOU'VE
STARTED
LET US THEREFORE NOT BE PARTED

DO NOT SPEND AND DO NOT LEND
CHANGE ME NOT TO PLEASE A FRIEND

NINE THAT SHAKE ARE TWO TOO MANY
SIX WILL NEVER GRANT YOU ANY

ROYAL NOT ROMAN STRAIGHT NOT SNUB
THAT'S THE POINT AND THAT'S THE RUB.

Harmony tipped the tea chest back again and settled
herself on it, the piece of paper in one hand, the old
dog dangling from the other. "Methodical. Be methodical," she muttered, and concentrated on the first
two lines.

Because the riddle was Uncle Ginger's, she began
by thinking the words referred to him.

"Well, I do 'wish to keep you near,' " she said, "or
rather I did." But I don't understand about sharing a
year. I'm ten and you must be about forty, I should
think. Unless it's just the last year on the date, like
me being born in 1973 and you in 1943."

She scratched her head and looked at the next part.

"Six times more what? And when I've started what?
And it's no good saying 'let us not be parted.' We
have been."

29

It was not until she came again to the third couplet that she realized the "I" in the first line of all was not Uncle Ginger but the coin itself, which, for some reason, she mustn't spend or lend or change even to please a friend.

"Ah! Now the first line's easy. Sharing a year must mean it's a 1973 fifty pence piece." She fished it out and it was.

"All right," she said to it. "You were made the year I was born. And I mustn't get rid of you. I still don't follow this 'six times more' business. And as for 'nine that shake are two too many' . . . nine whats? And 'shake' . . . let's see, you shake in your shoes if you're frightened, you shake with laughter, you shake your head to mean no, you shake . . . hands. Hands! There are hands—on the coin!"

She looked carefully at it. On the one side was the head of the queen facing toward her title—Elizabeth II—while behind the head was written D.G. Reg.F.D. And on the other side was a ring of hands, clasping one another, and inside the ring:

1973

50

PENCE

Quickly she counted the hands. "Nine! But those are two too many, it says. So seven. But six will never grant me any. So that leaves one. One what? One hand?"

30

She looked very attentively at the nine hands. Mostly they looked like men's hands, but one, the one just to the right of the fifty, was definitely a female hand.

"It must be something to do with that hand. That's the one that's going to grant me . . . what? What do you *grant*, Rex Ruff Monty?"

Harmony stood up and went out through the low door of the chicken house and, as she did so, she had the clearest picture of doing the same two weeks ago, and of the Silvertip coming out behind her and stretching himself and saying, "D'you do a lot of wishing, Harmony?"

Wishes. You grant wishes! In fairy stories, and stories of magic!

And she heard herself saying, "D'you know anything about magic? Yourself?" and his reply, "A bit."

It was a magic fifty pence piece, that would grant her wishes! That female hand was the key to it, that must be the answer.

Hastily she reread the end of the riddle. The next-to-the-last line didn't make any sense to her, but the last word of all did. "Rub." That's what she had to do.

Carefully Harmony laid Rex Ruff Monty down on the grass and put the piece of paper in her pocket. She held the coin in her left hand with the Queen's head facing downward and put the tip of her right forefinger on that feminine-looking hand. She closed her eyes tight. She thought of a whole host of possible wishes and decided to start with something simple. At that moment she heard the car coming up the drive as the shoppers returned, and that made her think it would soon be lunchtime. She would have her favorite lunch!

"I *wish*," said Harmony, "for fish sticks and baked beans and french fries and catsup," and she rubbed hard.

For twenty minutes she lay in the orchard grass and waited, her mind in a whirl of excitement, the fifty pence piece seeming almost to burn her hand with its magic powers. Then she heard the Pouter Pigeon's call, "Harmony! Lunch is ready."

Slowly Harmony walked up the orchard, in through the french windows, across the living room, and paused outside the dining room door, the coin clenched in her hand. She turned the handle and walked in.

It was cold meat and salad.

"Why aren't we having fish sticks?" she said.

"Harmony, what are you talking about?"

"You're disgusting, Harm. I suppose you expected baked beans and french fries and catsup too, on a boiling hot day like this?"

"Yes."

"Don't be silly, Harmony darling. And go and wash. Your hands are dirty."

"She's got something in one of her grubby paws, Mummy. What is it, Harm?"

"Mind your own stinking . . ."

"Harmony! You are not to speak to your sister like that. What have you got there?"

Harmony opened her hand.

"Little liar," said Melody, "you said you hadn't got any money. You said there wasn't any in the envelope. Imagine Uncle Ginger only giving her fifty pence, Mummy. My dress must have cost the earth." She unsheathed her claws for a final scratch. "Still, I suppose fifty pence's a lot for a kid like you."

Automatically, as she washed her hands, Harmony made the two appropriate faces, My Mother Drives Me Mad and I Hate My Sister, but she wasn't really thinking about either of them.

She ate her lunch at top speed and without tasting it, her thoughts concentrated on the riddle. All right, she hadn't found the answer, but not for a moment did she doubt the power of the coin. She slipped one hand into her pocket and fingered its straight edges. How many sides did a fifty pence piece have? Oh! Was the answer something to do with that?

"Your day for washing up, Harm," said the Siamese, dabbing her lips in a maddeningly delicate way.

Harmony wiped the back of her hand over her mouth and put on her Pleading Face, eyes very wide, head tipped a little to one side, eyebrows raised a pathetic fraction.

"Oh, Melody. You wouldn't like to swap, would you? Please? I've got something awfully important to do."

"Important? You? Yes, I'll swap."

"You will?"

"At a price."

"How much?"

"Fifty pence."

"Smelly flea-bitten cat!"

"Harmony! You are not to speak to your sister like that. And please don't bang those plates around, you'll break something.

The washing up finished and her bedroom door locked, Harmony counted the sides on the coin. Seven. She studied the paper.

" 'Six times more when once you've started.' One plus six equals seven.

"And the 'nine' line. Nine minus two equals seven.

34

"So it's to do with the sides, not the hands. But six sides won't grant me any wishes. Only one will, that's the point.

" 'That's the point'—it says so in the last line.

"So it all depends on, 'royal not Roman straight not snub.'

"Well, royal's easy enough, it's got something to do with the Queen's head. And straight, well, the coin's got straight sides, I suppose. I can't see where Roman comes in. Now I know what a snub is, it's when someone tries to make you feel small or stupid, like Simple Sissie's always doing to me. But I can't see the point of it here. Perhaps it's got something to do with D.G.Reg.F.D. around the side of the coin. If only I knew what that meant. I suppose you don't by any chance know, R.R.M.?"

Rex Ruff Monty's single eye seemed expressionless but it appeared to tell Harmony something.

"Of course," she said, "you're right as usual. All I've got to do is to rub each side in turn and wish, and if the wish comes true I've got the right one." But somehow that seemed to be almost like cheating, and not the right way to solve the riddle. With the patience—stubbornness, her family called it—that was part of her nature, Harmony decided to wait until her father came home. She would pick his brains. After all, she thought, he's the only one with any brains to pick.

Mr. Parker usually arrived back from the city around

six o'clock. Harmony had never really known what he did for a living. Because of her picture of him she imagined him balancing a big, colored rubber ball on the end of his nose or playing the national anthem on a row of squeaky horns and then clapping his flippers together and barking. Sometimes the picture was so vivid that she was quite surprised to see he had two legs.

As usual, the Sea Lion dropped into his special armchair while the Pouter Pigeon fluttered off to bring him his special drink and the Siamese Cat purred and rubbed herself against his shiny black suit. Harmony did not normally take part in this welcoming ceremony, so he was a little surprised to find her standing beside him wearing a somewhat strange look. This was in fact her Seeker After Knowledge Face, earnest, serious, attentive, respectful.

"Harmony," grunted the Sea Lion. "What is the matter? You do not look your usual self."

"What's D.G.Reg.F.D.?" said Harmony.

"What on earth are you talking about?"

"On a fifty pence piece. Have you got a fifty pence piece?"

Understanding dawned in the Sea Lion's rather prominent eyes. He felt in his pocket and produced the first coin that came to hand, a two pence piece as it happened. "My dear Harmony," he said, "I'm surprised you haven't noticed that these letters appear on every coin of the realm. They stand for 'Dei gratia Regina fidei defensor.' "

36

"What's that mean?"

"It means, 'By the grace of God, Queen, defender of the faith.' "

"What language is that?"

Mr. Parker sighed. "Latin, Harmony, Latin. The language of the ancient Romans."

Royal not Roman, thought Harmony, straight not snub.

"If you snub someone," she said, "it means you make them feel silly, doesn't it?"

The Sea Lion looked suspicious. He had had his flipper pulled before now.

"My dear Harmony, I was not snubbing you, merely trying to blow away a little of the mists of ignorance through which you peer at the world."

"No, I meant—does 'snub" mean anything else?"

"Of course. It means 'turned up.' Of a nose. The opposite to a Roman nose."

A great sunburst of light shone through the mists of ignorance. With the discretion—coldness, her family called it—that was part of her nature, Harmony gave no outward sign of the excitement bubbling up inside her.

"Thanks," she said.

"Crossword puzzle or something, was it?" asked Mr. Parker, shaking out his evening paper.

"Sort of," she said, and to her father's great surprise she kissed him on the top of his bald head.

Safely in her room, wearing the Ridiculously Happy

37

Face, she read the riddle once again. At last it was all clear. This particular 1973 fifty pence piece would give her in all (said the second couplet) seven wishes. She must never part with it. As she had guessed, the fourth couplet told that only one of its seven sides was the magic one. And the last two lines told her which one.

Royal not Roman straight not snub. That was the Queen's Nose!! The side at which the Queen's Nose pointed, that was the magic side!

This time Harmony did not shut her eyes. She held the coin with the Queen's head upward and began to rub the magic side, backward and forward, from the "I" to the "T" of ELIZABETH and back again, slowly at first, and then faster and faster until the metal edge began to feel warm beneath her finger.

"I *wish*," said Harmony, "for an animal. Of my very own."

Downstairs, the front doorbell rang.

CHAPTER 4

"What Will You Wish Today?"

Harmony and Melody arrived at the door together. Outside stood a figure that they saw in two different ways. Melody saw the local traffic warden, a small man with a stringy neck, a wide unsmiling mouth, and glassy unblinking eyes. He wore his dark uniform and cap with a yellow stripe.

Harmony saw a Great Crested Newt.

There was no doubt, however, as to what he was carrying. It was a middle-sized white rabbit with black spots.

"Better put it back in its hutch before it gets run over," said the Newt severely.

"It doesn't belong here," said Melody.

At that moment Mr. Parker came to the door.

"My car parked wrongly?" he asked.

You're a bad Parker, thought Harmony, and she made her Private Joke Face, shoulders hunched, neck shortened, ears waggling.

The Newt shot her a cold amphibious glance.

"No, nothing like that, sir," he said. "I was just going off duty when I saw this rabbit out in the road. And then all of a sudden it came straight in through your front gate and up the path to the door. Just as

though someone had called it. So I thought . . ."

"Very kind of you," barked the Sea Lion, "but it doesn't belong to us."

Quickly Harmony put on her Pleading Face, and the Newt saw his chance.

"Perhaps one of your little girls would like to look after it?"

The Siamese Cat stalked off at being called a little girl, and Harmony turned the Pleading Face full on her father.

"Just for the night?" she said. "Just till the real owner comes along?" You cannot refuse, she thought. You cannot resist the power of the Queen's Nose.

The Sea Lion looked at her. He passed a flipper over the top of his shiny pate. Perhaps the memory of that rare and unexpected kiss that it had received may have influenced him, but he heard himself saying, "Well, just for the night. But I'm not having the smelly thing in the house, d'you understand?" and he humped himself back to his drink and his paper.

His smooth face empty of expression, the Newt handed over his burden and slid away down the street, pale eyes flicking from side to side at the lines of silent cars. Harmony stood watching him for a moment, the rabbit cradled in her arms. She wore her Ridiculously Happy Face. She kept it on as she walked around through the front garden into the orchard, and down to her den, until the effort of maintaining the grin made her cheeks ache.

Inside the chicken house, she sat on the tea chest

and watched as the rabbit hopped around the floor, puckering up its nose at the strange smells. She fetched some dandelions and it began to eat, sitting at her feet. It seemed completely at home.

"An animal. Of my very own," said Harmony aloud. "I just wished it, and it happened."

She took the fifty pence piece out of her pocket and absentmindedly rubbed the magic edge.

"I *wish* Uncle Ginger knew that I'd solved the riddle," she said without thinking. Almost before she had time to realize what she'd done, she heard her name called.

"Harmony! Where are you? It's Uncle Ginger on the phone. He wants to speak to you."

"What did you want?" said the Silvertip Grizzly's deep voice as soon as she picked the instrument up. Harmony glanced hastily round the room. The Siamese's ears were pricked, she could see that right away. She could not see the Sea Lion's small ones for he was wallowing behind his newspaper, and the Pouter's were hidden beneath the neat feathering of her hair; but it was obvious that they were listening.

"Thank you very much for the money," she said.

"I hope it will come in . . . useful."

"Oh, it has."

"So I gathered. I got the message pretty clear, just a few minutes ago."

"Oh."

"I think you've wasted a wish, haven't you?"

"Yes. I mean no, it's lovely to hear from you."

"Was that the first wish you'd made? Just now?"

"No."

"You sound as though the rest of the family were all listening like mad."

"Yes."

"You know how many you've got, don't you? Wishes, I mean?"

"Yes."

"Well, don't waste any more, will you?"

"No."

"When you've finished your absolutely riveting conversation, composed entirely as it is of 'Yes' and 'No,' " said Mr. Parker, "perhaps I could have a word."

"I'll have to go now, Uncle Ginger," said Harmony. "I think Daddy wants to talk to you. By the way, I've got a rabbit."

As she went out through the french windows she heard the Sea Lion's bark. . . . "Hullo? Ginger? Good trip? What? No, of course she hasn't been given one . . . somebody brought the mangy thing to the door . . . put it somewhere overnight . . . have to go to the pet shop if no one claims it."

"But no one will claim you," said Harmony, back on the tea chest. "And you will not go to the pet shop. You'll see. Now, we must find you a name. You look to be female somehow. Of course! You're Anita!"

Though they were unaware of it, all the children in Harmony's class at school were animals of one kind

43

or another. A lamb might sit at the same table with a lion, sharing it perhaps with a porcupine or a parrot or even (for Harmony's knowledge of natural history was wide) with a Leadbeater's Possum or a Colombian Douracouli. And as soon as she had set eyes on this rather fat little girl with sticking-out teeth and hair worn in two high bunches like ears, Harmony had imagined her nibbling at a head of lettuce held in her paws. So if Anita was a rabbit, the rabbit should be Anita.

By bedtime Anita looked very comfortable. Harmony had cut a sheaf of long dry grass to make a bed; she had filled a bowl with water; and she had put out a kind of cafeteria in the nest boxes: a crust snitched from the breadbox, some carrots pinched from the vegetable patch, a fallen apple, and more dandelions.

She told Rex Ruff Monty about it in great detail as they lay in bed and watched the moon coming up through the trees. He did not comment, but she was sure he was happy for her. And there were still five wishes to go! She fell asleep in the blink of a rabbit's eye.

Her first thought on waking, quite early, was for Anita. She dressed and ran down through the dewy orchard, the old dog dangling from her hand.

On a top branch a thrush sang his repeating song. "What will you *wish* today? What will you *wish* today?" Harmony could hear the words clearly.

Anita and Rex Ruff Monty were introduced, with-

out much interest on either side, and then Harmony
let the rabbit out. The orchard was fenced on three
sides, so that it could not escape next door, or onto
the road; the worst it could do was to go toward the
house and onto the lawn. She soon found that she
could herd it quite easily as it grazed.

Soon there came the whine of the milkman's truck,
and then his head peeped over the top of the roadside
fence. To the average eye, he was a small, chirpy,
yellow-headed man with a little pointed nose. He
whistled constantly. To Harmony of course he was a
Canary.

"Hullo," said the Canary. "You're up early this
morning."

"I'm pasturing my rabbit," said Harmony.

The Canary stood on his thin toes and pointed his
beak over the fence. Anita hopped toward him.

"What's it called?" he chirruped.

"Anita."

"What a lovely name," said the Canary, "and what a lovely rabbit."

"And what a lovely Canary you are," said Harmony under her breath as he fluttered off and trilled his happy way from house to house.

The tinkle of milk bottles set down on steps started Harmony thinking of other things that milkmen carry, like cream and eggs and yogurt.

"I'm hungry," she said to Anita, "and you've had quite enough for now." She picked the rabbit up and carried it back to the chicken house.

"Come on," she said to Rex Ruff Monty, "it must be time for breakfast," but when she looked up toward the house the curtains were still drawn. I wish I had a watch, she thought, and then she suddenly realized . . . you can, you can wish it! I can't imagine how it will happen, but it will! If you want a watch, just wish on the Queen's Nose!

Quickly she took the fifty pence piece out of the pocket of her jeans and turned it around so that the magic side was ready for her forefinger. She looked around to see if anyone was watching, but the only person in sight was the postman, at the end of the road.

To anyone else, that is, he was a postman. To Harmony, partly of course because of his pouch in which he carried the letters, partly because of his thick, strong-

46

looking legs and rather sheeplike face, he was a Kangaroo.

Harmony put on her Concentrated Thought Face.

"Right," she said. She half opened one eye to be sure that her finger was in the right place, and began to rub.

"I *wish*," said Harmony, "for a large wristwatch, digital, that tells you the month and the date as well, with a wide leather strap all mottled to look like snakeskin."

She waited a moment and then stared fixedly at her left wrist. She was concentrating so hard on it that at first she did not hear the voice from the footpath beyond the fence.

"Good morning," said the Kangaroo again.

"Oh . . . sorry. Good morning."

"You live here?" said the Kangaroo, pointing toward the house.

"Yes."

"Name of Parker?"

"Yes."

"You can take your mail if you like. Save my feet."

Harmony was not tall enough to look over the fence but she could imagine his feet all right, terribly strong and long and bony with sharp nails. She reached up and took some letters and a package.

"Thanks," said the Kangaroo. "I'll be hopping along now."

Absently, Harmony looked at the mail. There were

47

three letters for the Sea Lion, one for the Pouter Pigeon, and a picture postcard for the Siamese. Idly, she turned the package over. It was for her.

Carefully, terribly carefully, Harmony put the coin back in her pocket. With hands that trembled quite a lot she somehow undid the string and tape that bound the package. Inside the brown paper was a blue box. Inside the blue box was white tissue paper. And inside the white tissue paper was a large wristwatch, digital, with the month on it, and the date, and a wide leather strap all mottled to look like snakeskin.

CHAPTER 5

The Icebreaker

At breakfast, Harmony's parents seemed not to notice. Stolidly they ate and read their letters while Harmony continually passed her left wrist beneath their very noses in a series of extravagant gestures to reach toast or butter or marmalade. She had begun by eating her cornflakes left-handed, holding the spoon to her mouth for long periods, the face of the watch presented to each in turn. It was not until Melody's late arrival that it was noticed.

"Where *did* you get that from?" she said.

"It came in the mail."

"Who from?"

"Uncle Ginger." (There had been no letter in the blue box but Harmony recognized the printed capitals on the address, done with a black Magic Marker just like those on the treasure hunt notes. And there was a Devonshire postmark.)

"Very nice," and, "How kind of him," came absently from the others, but the Siamese could not resist a scratch.

"How stupid," she said in her cattiest voice as she sat down opposite. "It's a boy's watch, a man's watch, I should say. It just looks silly on you."

Harmony had a useful alternative to the look that signified I Hate My Sister. It was the I Love (To Kick) My Sister Face. She put it on, suited the action to it, and was through the door in a flash, Melody's yell of agony ringing pleasantly in her ears.

Safely at the bottom of the orchard—there would be no pursuit, she knew, for fear of ambush—she lay in the grass between the still form of Rex Ruff Monty and the busy, hopping, nibbling Anita, and watched time pass. What an *ace* watch it was! And still four more wishes to go. She felt the fifty pence piece in her pocket. With her thumb, she found, she could feel the roughness of the fingers on the clasped hands and so turn it to bring the royal head uppermost. More, her own finger was sensitive enough to feel the shape of that head, to locate the Queen's Nose. Like a gunfighter, she began to practice drawing the coin. Her pocket was the holster, the magic edge the trigger that would send another wish speeding unerringly to its target. Soon she could place that trigger finger opposite the Queen's Nose almost every time. The fastest gun in the West, thought Harmony, but remember, only four bullets left.

When, at the end of Anita's grazing time, she made her way back up to the house, she went with caution. More Indian than cowboy, she slipped from tree to tree, crossed the lawn like a shadow, and glided toward the stairs, intent on reaching the safety of her room before an avenging Siamese might pounce. The

Sea Lion had gone to the city to perform his tricks, and the Pouter, she saw as she tiptoed through the hall, was writing a letter. The bottom stair creaked under her weight, and she heard her mother call her name.

Harmony put on her Here We Go Again Face, lower lip stuck out, eyebrows high, eyes rolling wildly.

"Yes, Mummy?"

Mrs. Parker, however, was easily able to forget things that had happened only a short time ago. Pigeonlike, the sound of her own voice pleased her most, and far more earthshaking events than a mere squabble between her daughters could pass her by unnoticed. Occasionally, annoyingly, she remembered awkward things, and this was one of those occasions.

"That fifty pence piece that Uncle Ginger gave you."

"Yes?"

"You haven't spent it, have you?"

"No."

"Oh, good. I've got to pop down to the post office and I'm out of stamps and there'll be a line a mile long—it's the day people get their pension checks—but there's a machine outside that sells a fifty pence book. So if I give you five tens . . ."

"But, Mummy . . ."

"Yes?"

"I . . . don't want to . . . I mean I can't . . . I mean, this one's special."

"Oh, don't be silly, Harmony, five tens will buy you exactly the same. I'll tell you what, the next time

I have a fifty pence you can change the tens back again. After all, one fifty pence piece is just the same as another, you know. Come along, darling, I'm in a hurry," and Mrs. Parker counted five coins and held them out.

Afterward Harmony thought of all the ways she could have dodged the issue. She could have offered to run the errand herself and changed the tens at a shop on the way. She could have volunteered to stand in the line to get the stamps. She could simply have taken to her heels. As it was, she reacted instinctively. Cornered, she went for her gun.

All in one lightning movement she put her hand into her pocket, felt for the royal face and rubbed.

"I *wish* you didn't need this particular fifty pence," she said.

Melody limped into the room.

"Oh, Melody darling," cried the Pouter plaintively, "I need a fifty pence piece for a book of stamps, can you help me? Harmony won't, I can't think why."

"Of course, Mummy," purred the Siamese. "I'm sure I've got one in my purse. I'll go and fetch it. Some people are selfish little beasts."

I've wasted another one, thought Harmony. But when she looked she could see that her finger had been rubbing at the back of the Queen's head. This time it was not magic that had saved her but just ordinary luck.

In her bedroom Harmony sat by the window and

turned the magic coin from side to side in the light.
You could change the Queen's expression, she found,
by tipping that nose toward you and away from you.
You could make her look sad, then start a small smile
that turned into a grin, and then into an expression
that was at first serious and finally severe.

She tried all the different faces herself in front of
the looking glass. When she came to the severe one,
she kept it on and addressed herself in harsh tones.

"What would the Silvertip think if he knew you'd nearly thrown away another one? Here you are, with a magic coin that can grant you anything you want, anything. You must make absolutely sure, the next time, that you get something you really need, something you simply couldn't have without this magic power. Now think, Harmony, think hard," and she changed the Severe Queen for the Concentrated Thought. She must choose something sensible and useful, something that cost so much that she would never normally have thought of it.

Of course! A bike! Not a handed down, bashed up, bent and rusty thing like her present one, but a brand-new one, sparkling, brilliant, unbelievably expensive! She could see them all now, a great army of them paraded for her inspection in the window of the big bicycle stores in the shopping center, all shapes, all sizes, all colors of the rainbow. Any one she liked was hers for the wishing!

"We'll go now, Rex Ruff Monty," she said.

"How? On the bus of course.

"Have I got money for the fare, you say? I think so."

Quickly she pulled the rubber plug out of the china pig inside whose pink potbelly lay all her worldly wealth, and counted her money.

There was enough, just.

"After all, we shan't need a return ticket!"

She ran downstairs. Melody was lying on the sofa in the living room, painting her claws a horrid shade of green. It was about the same color, Harmony noticed with some satisfaction, as the bruise on her leg.

"Where's Mummy?" she said.

"Gone to the post office, you selfish little beast."

"Tell her I'm going shopping."

"Shopping? You? Going to spend that fifty pence piece you were too selfish to change for her, I suppose."

In the bus Harmony handed over a collection of halfpennies and pennies and two-pence pieces to the driver (an Old English Sheepdog, she noted with interest), and sat, tense with excitement, Rex Ruff Monty in one hand, the other gripping the magic coin in her pocket. One or two people stared curiously at the small girl with the battered toy dog, but a quick display of the Private Joke Face made them look hastily away.

When she reached the bicycle shop, she stood outside for a long time, and gazed. How would she ever choose? They were all so beautiful. There were tall bikes with thin tires and short, stubby bikes with thick ones. There were bikes with drooping handlebars like charging rams, and bikes with handlebars that swept up like ibexes' horns. There were blue bikes, red bikes, green bikes, yellow bikes. And they were all gloriously, shiningly . . . new!

Harmony went inside and stood among them. Perhaps it was the quiet and coolness behind the plate glass, perhaps the bright exotic colors of the silent inhabitants, but she felt as though she were inside an aquarium. She was therefore not surprised to see that the salesman who moved noiselessly toward her over the sandy-tinted floor was unmistakably a Sea Trout. Spotty and sleek, his yellow eyes bright, he hovered beside her.

"Can I help you, young lady?"

"I want a bike," said Harmony.

"Ah," said the Sea Trout. He cast a fishy look at this customer's scruffy, chopped-off jeans, old canvas shoes, and none-too-clean "Save the Whale" T-shirt.

"Which one did you fancy?"

Harmony hesitated as he patted the nearest, a slim speed machine with handles that almost touched the floor.

"Well, this one for example," he said, "is a racing model, twenty-eight-inch wheels, caliper brakes, dynohub lighting, twelve-speed gears. Is that what you had in mind perhaps?"

"No," said Harmony. "I want one with fat tires. And sensible handlebars, not ones that stick up or hang down. And a saddlebag. For my dog."

The Sea Trout goggled at Rex Ruff Monty.

"I see," he said. "How about these then? Quite a different type of machine. Twenty-inch wheels, three speeds, chain guard, reflectors on the end of the hand-grips, padded safety strut between the handlebars. And the tires arc certainly, er, fat. Very popular, with boys especially."

There were three of these side by side, all much alikc. One was a "Firefly," brilliant red. The second was a "Thunderbolt," all yellow and silver. And the third was blue, a dark mysterious blue the color of some cold secret lake. It had a box-shaped container, just the right size, above its rear wheel. It was called "Icebreaker." Harmony pointed to it.

"I'll take that one, please."

"Don't you want to know how much it is?"

"How much is it?"

"A hundred and forty pounds."

"All right."

Harmony put her hand in her pocket and drew out the fifty pence piece.

She felt for the Queen's Nose and found the magic edge. She rubbed.

"I *wish*," she said in a voice of quiet command, "to have this bike."

The Sea Trout gulped. He called to a lady assistant (a Goldfish, Harmony could see).

"This young lady," he said, "wishes to purchase this model. I have told her the price. I'm afraid fifty pence's not going to go very far."

The Goldfish's eyes bulged.

"*This* model?" she said, touching the Icebreaker on its black plastic saddle, stuck in the middle of which, Harmony could see, was a large red star. "This *particular* model?"

"Yes."

"Excuse us a moment, dear," said the Goldfish to Harmony, and she drew the Sea Trout away. Harmony could see her thick lips move as she whispered to him. They went behind the counter and there the Goldfish pressed a bell.

Out from some secret cave at the back of the aquarium there swam into view a ponderous gray shape with very large spectacles that seemed to stick out on either side—a Hammerhead Shark, without a doubt—and all three conferred together.

At last the Hammerhead Shark approached Harmony.

"Good morning, my dear," he said in an oily voice. "I am the manager of this shop. I understand that you wish to purchase this beautiful bicycle?"

"Yes, please."

"You know its price?"

"Yes. The Sea Tr . . . the man told me."

"Wherever would you find all that money?"

Silly old Shark, thought Harmony. You cannot resist the power of the Queen's Nose.

"Please, may I have it now?" she asked politely.

The Hammerhead Shark shook his hammer head in amazed disbelief.

Behind him, the Sea Trout and the Goldfish shook theirs.

"You are a very, very lucky young lady," he said.

"Yes. I know."

"This bicycle," he said, and he picked the Ice-breaker out of its stand and set it reverently down before Harmony in all its blue beauty, "this bicycle that you have chosen is no ordinary bicycle. This bicycle—as the red star on its saddle tells—is very different from any other bicycle, or any model, in this shop, in this town, in the whole of England. Not even my assistants knew this—this lady here merely had orders to call me should any customer select the machine with the red star on its saddle—but this bicycle is the ten . . . thousandth . . . Icebreaker to be made."

"Oh," said Harmony.

"And because it is the ten . . . thousandth . . . model," boomed the Hammerhead Shark, his voice growing louder and louder as he continued, "that very famous firm of cycle manufacturers from whose workshops it came"—he mentioned a nationally known name—"decided in their wisdom that for the purposes of advertising the customer fortunate enough to select this particular bicycle"—he patted the red-starred saddle—"should be offered it, not at trade price, not at half price, but"—he paused and threw wide his arms—"FREE!!!"

Harmony put the fifty pence piece back in the pocket of her jeans.

"Thanks," she said.

CHAPTER 6

Gentlemen of the Press

The granting of all the wishes so far had been so instant, so immediate, that Harmony expected just to jump on the Icebreaker and ride away home. However, this particular result of the magic of the Queen's Nose was not to be had quite so easily. To her dismay she found that she had acquired not just a bicycle but fame as well.

This was the moment that the Hammerhead Shark had been eagerly awaiting, ever since the manufacturers had chosen his shop for their advertising gimmick. For two whole weeks now the Icebreaker had stood in his window with that telltale red star on its saddle. Many children, with or without their parents, had looked at it. Several had wanted it, chosen it even, only to change their minds or have their minds changed, and pick a different model. Now at last a child had decided upon it, and he was determined to wring the maximum publicity from the occasion.

A pity, thought the Hammerhead, regarding Harmony narrowly out of his small hard eyes, that it had to be this child. The machine was far more suitable for a boy. He had imagined the lucky owner as a strapping lad, neatly dressed, smiling broadly for the photographers, brimming over with happiness at his good fortune.

Instead, here was this scruffy girl who seemed to be taking the whole thing as a matter of course. He could see no glint of excitement in her large brown eyes. It was almost as though she had expected to receive a bicycle worth a hundred and forty pounds for nothing. With only fifty pence in her pocket!

He was certainly going to be in no hurry to hand it over until he knew a great deal more about her. And he must contact the press right away. He smiled a cold shark's smile.

"Aren't you a lucky girl?" he said.

"Yes," said Harmony. "Can I have the bike now? I ought to start riding home or I'll be late for lunch and Mummy will start worrying."

"Oh, we can't have Mummy worrying," said the Hammerhead. "I tell you what we'll do—what is your name, by the way?"

"Harmony Parker."

"I'll tell you what we'll do, Harmony—what a pretty name—we'll ring up Mummy and tell her what a lucky, lucky daughter she's got. And then, soon, you'll be able to take your lovely new bike away."

"Why can't I take it now?"

The Hammerhead Shark laughed, showing rows of large teeth. Behind him the Goldfish giggled and the Sea Trout simpered.

"Oh, goodness me, it's not quite as simple as that. You're going to be quite famous, you see. It's not

every day that something like this happens, is it? You're going to have your picture in the papers, you know. The local papers and, I hope, the national papers. You might even be on television. You'll like that, won't you? Now, you tell me where you live and your telephone number and we'll get everything fixed up."

Harmony put her hand in her pocket and fingered the Queen's Nose. She did not like the Hammerhead Shark and she did not want to be famous. I could soon make you hand it over without any of this fuss, she thought. But there were only three wishes left. She gave her address and number.

Within a very short space of time the bicycle shop was overflowing with people. Mrs. Parker and Melody arrived, there were reporters and photographers, and a crowd of curious passersby gazed through the windows. Harmony was photographed standing by the Icebreaker, sitting on the Icebreaker, shaking hands with a beaming Hammerhead Shark as the Icebreaker was formally presented to her.

"Smile, dear!" cried the photographers, but one glimpse of the Ridiculously Happy Face soon stopped that.

"Solemn . . . self-contained . . . dazed by her good fortune, little Harmony Parker showed no emotion . . ." scribbled the reporters.

"Oh, what does she look like in those dreadful old clothes!" pouted Mrs. Parker to Melody, but Melody was too busy trying to get into the picture.

Before the final shots were taken—of Harmony riding away up the street—the lucky owner of the ten thousandth Icebreaker was interviewed by the gentlemen of the press. They must have believed everything that was said to them by this wide-eyed child, for the reports in the following day's newspapers read strangely to the eyes of her family.

The Sea Lion, traveling early as usual to his office, learned that he was not, as he had thought these many years, an ordinary undistinguished businessman, but a chartered accountant of the highest repute.

("And where does your Daddy work?"

"In the city."

"What does he do?"

"Oh, some pretty clever tricks. He balances things, I always imagine."

"Balances things? Oh, balances the books, you mean? I see! And he's brilliant, is he?"

"Ace.")

The Pouter Pigeon, arriving late to breakfast as usual, found herself described as an interesting invalid, suffering from a rare complaint.

("And what does Mummy do?"

"Nothing much."

"Nothing? Why is that?"

"She's not much good at anything, I suppose. She lies down quite a lot."

"Lies down? Ah, she needs rest? What is the matter with her?"

"I can't say. She's always been like that."

"Always, eh? Tragic, tragic!")

But the Siamese Cat fared worst of all. Somehow the reporters must have misheard Harmony's pronunciation of her name. Somehow they must have misinterpreted the rather vacuous open-mouthed smiles with which Melody greeted their every glance across the shop, hoping as she did that someone would photograph her. Or maybe they just misunderstood what Harmony said.

("So that's your sister?"

"Yes."

"What a strange name. Do you call her that or have you a special nickname for her?"

"I call her Simple Sissie."

"Simple, eh? Oh, dear.")

Whatever the reason, the morning paper sent the

elder Miss Parker into screaming hysterics.

Beneath a picture of Harmony astride the Ice-breaker, she read:

LITTLE GIRL'S STROKE OF LUCK.
The Ten Thousandth Bike—Free!

Harmony Parker, younger daughter of a brilliant London chartered accountant, yesterday became the proud owner of the 10,000th Icebreaker to be manufactured. . . .

There followed details of the bike itself and the story of the mysterious red star on its saddle ("How many children, I wonder, must be wishing now that they had made that choice"), and of course mention by name both of the Hammerhead Shark and of his shop.

It was the last sentence, however, that set the Siamese yowling.

> Little Harmony Parker will have other uses for her treasured new possession than merely joyriding, for she will be able to pedal away on many an errand for her family.
>
> Her mother, alas, is a chronic invalid, condemned to rest for much of the day. And her sister, Malady, copes bravely with the problems of backwardness.

CHAPTER 7

Lost and Found

For several days after this Harmony hardly thought about the Queen's Nose. She seemed to be so busy, going for long rides on the Icebreaker with Rex Ruff Monty tucked up in the blue saddlebag behind her. He just fitted nicely, provided she folded his soft leg under him. And then there was the watch to consult, frequently, to make sure she was back in good time to give Anita her proper ration of grazing and play. Always the magic coin was in the pocket of those old jeans, and every so often she would touch it just to reassure herself. But she wasn't tempted to use it yet. Vague ideas were forming in her head for the last three wishes, but she was in no hurry. There were still three weeks of the summer holidays left.

She had just returned from a ride when the Pouter Pigeon came fluttering out to meet her in the drive.

"Harmony darling, you'll never guess what's happened!"

"What?"

"You're going to be on television! The BBC called and said could they come out and interview you tomorrow!"

"Oh, no, Mummy. You didn't say yes, did you?"

"Of course! And one thing I absolutely insist on. You are not going in front of the cameras wearing those awful clothes. We'll go out this afternoon and buy you a pretty new dress."

Harmony said nothing. Instead she put on her No Torture On Earth Can Make Me Do What You Say Face. From long experience Mrs. Parker immediately recognized this and lowered her sights.

"Well, some nice new jeans then."

"Can I choose them?"

"Yes."

"And a new T-shirt?"

"Yes."

"And a pair of running shoes? And soccer socks?"

"Soccer socks! Darling, you can't . . . oh, very well."

So it came about the following evening that a few million viewers watched on their television screens an item about a small girl who had been given a new bicycle. Harmony had considered using the Queen's Nose to keep the television crew away, but somehow that didn't seem fair once she had put on her new clothes, so she had gone through with the interview stoically.

She wore an emerald-green T-shirt emblazoned with the message "Furs Are for Animals not People" in scarlet capital letters, bright pink jeans tucked into brilliant red-and-gold striped soccer socks, and on her feet running shoes with black and sky-blue stripes.

After the interviewer and the electrician and the

cameraman had packed up and left the Parkers' house
that morning, Harmony kept on her new clothes all
afternoon. She was wearing them still as they all sat
around the television and watched her looking out at
them from the screen in her motley. Thousands of
viewers were doubtless adjusting the color on their
sets.

When it was over, they commented in their fashion.

"You only seemed to say Yes and No, darling—I
wish you'd said more."

"Be thankful that she did not."

"You looked a complete freak, Harm—you'd have been better in your usual old rags," said Melody, and went out of the room.

Later on, Harmony suddenly felt she needed her usual old rags. All day they'd lain on the chair in her bedroom, the magic coin in the pocket of the sawed-off jeans, and Rex Ruff Monty guarding it.

The moment she opened the door she felt a thrill of horror. Rex Ruff Monty was there, the old T-shirt was there, the canvas shoes were there. The jeans were gone.

She dashed downstairs two at a time.

"Mummy! Where are my old jeans?"

The Pouter edged a little closer to the Sea Lion for support.

"I'm afraid they're gone. They were really too revolting."

"Gone? Where?"

"I put them in the trash."

Harmony shot away in a flash of color, through the hall, across the kitchen, out to the little yard at the back. The Queen's Nose in the trash indeed! Good thing the garbagemen didn't come till Monday. She ripped off the lid. The trash can was empty.

She walked slowly back to the living room. Normally she would have been wearing the My Mother Drives Me Mad Face, but this was too serious.

"The garbagemen must have come," she said in a very quiet voice.

"Yes, they have, darling. Next Monday's a Bank Holiday, you see, so they came early this week."

"Do you mean to say that you threw away my old jeans without even looking in the pockets?"

"Of course not, darling. Of course I looked. There was a hanky in one of them—I've washed it."

"What about the other pocket?"

"Oh, I'm afraid there was only one thing in that," said Mrs. Parker with a giggle.

"Yes?"

"A hole in the bottom of it."

Ten minutes later Harmony was sitting on the tea chest in the chicken house, Rex Ruff Monty swinging in her hand, while Anita snuffled curiously at the red-

and-gold striped soccer socks. She had already searched her bedroom floor. She wore the Concentrated Thought Face.

What did I do this morning between getting up and changing for the BBC people? I had it last thing last night, I know, playing with it. (Often Harmony would lie in bed and play a game with the magic coin, indulging herself in fantastic wishes—I *wish* I was on the Moon, I *wish* I had black hair and blue eyes. I *wish* I could play striker for England—while always being careful to rub any of the other six sides but never the one at which the Queen's Nose pointed.) So where could it have fallen out? In here. Anywhere in the orchard when I was pasturing you, Anita. Bathroom, stairs, kitchen, dining room, living room.

All evening she searched, high and low, but of the magic coin there was no sign.

"I *wish* I could find you," said Harmony miserably, when at last she lay in bed, but without the power of the Queen's Nose her wish, she knew, was just as futile as anyone else's.

She thought of the riddle. "You will wish to keep me near." I am wishing like mad, but where are you? And, "Let us therefore not be parted." But we have been.

"Oh, dear," sighed Harmony in Rex Ruff Monty's ear. "And to think there are three left. I tell you what. If anyone finds it, I'll jolly well give them one of those three wishes, and that's a solemn promise and you're my witness."

74

For a long time she could not get to sleep, and when she did her dreams were all of fifty pence pieces. Anita had them for eyes, the watch had one as a face, the bicycle's wheels were fifty pence pieces.

She slept late and was last down to breakfast.

"What exactly were you up to yesterday evening?" asked the Sea Lion, polishing off a kipper.

"Yes," said the Pouter Pigeon, pecking at her cornflakes, "what were you doing, darling? Wandering all over the house staring at the floor, and tramping up and down the orchard."

"I lost something."

"What?"

"A fifty pence piece."

The Siamese Cat looked up from her milk.

"Oh, not that old fifty pence piece, was it? Was that what you were turning the place upside down for? Why didn't you say so?"

"What d'you mean?"

"It was on your bedroom floor. I saw it there as I went past your door, right after your famous T.V. appearance. It must have dropped through that hole in your pocket—when Mummy took those revolting trousers of yours away."

"What did you do with it?"

"What do you imagine I did with it—spent it? I'm not a thief, you know, Harm, whatever else you may think of me," said Melody rather bitterly.

"Well, where is it?"

75

"Where it should have been all the time. I put it in that hideous pink piggy bank of yours."

Before she could move, Melody found herself enveloped in a bear hug of Silvertip strength and felt upon her cheek, of all things, a kiss.

"Oh, thanks, Melody, thanks a million!" cried Harmony, and was gone from the room like a whirlwind.

Utter amazement showed in the faces of her family.

"Whatever was all that about?" said her mother.

"Do not expect me to understand your younger daughter," said her father.

"All that fuss," said her sister, "about a perfectly ordinary old fifty pence piece. Whatever next?"

Later that morning she was to find out.

As soon as Harmony had unplugged the piggy bank and the precious coin was in the pocket of the new jeans—a pocket that she had turned inside out to make

sure that the stitching was strong and safe—she remembered her promise.

"Simple Sissie shall have the next wish," she said
to Rex Ruff Monty, "but we mustn't give away the
secret. I'm sure the Silvertip wouldn't approve of that.
I'll have to wish it for her. I'll have to find out what
she wants."

Melody was lying on the sofa, reading an American
magazine, when she heard her name called.

"What d'you want?" she said.

"That's just what I was going to ask you."

"How d'you mean?"

"Well—just suppose you could have one wish. What would you wish for?"

"Oh, don't be silly, Harm. You can't get things just by wishing for them—that's babyish."

"But suppose you could—by magic. What would you wish for?"

"You are a baby. Imagine believing in magic. That's rubbish."

"Oh, go on, Melody. Just for fun. What would you?"

Melody clicked her teeth in annoyance. She wanted to be left in peace. She frowned and turned back to her magazine.

"Oh, I don't know."

"Go on. What would you?"

"Oh, for goodness sake! I'd . . . wish I could go to America."

In the chicken house Harmony discussed the matter with Rex Ruff Monty and Anita.

"It's not that it can't be done, you understand. The Queen's Nose can do anything. It's just that we must think carefully how to put it. I mean if I just say 'I wish Melody to go to America' like that, it might mean forever. Not that that would be so bad, but it wouldn't really be fair to Mummy and Daddy. And after all," she said, holding the fifty pence piece up to the light, "she did find you." She tipped it, and the Queen smiled at her.

In the end the form of words that she decided upon was so long that she had to go to her room and write it all down. She locked the piece of paper in the drawer where she kept her scrapbook, and decided that she would wait until after lunch, in fact until after she'd had a good long ride on the Icebreaker, and then look at it again and see if it seemed right.

After tea she did and it did. So she sat on the bed and rubbed the edge opposite the Queen's Nose and said, "I *wish* that my elder sister, Melody Parker, could go—provided she doesn't stay away from home too long and provided it doesn't cost her any money— to America."

She put the coin in her pocket and lay back on the bed, thinking about the two wishes that remained. Downstairs the telephone was ringing and she heard her mother's voice answering it. Then she heard her call Melody; and Melody's voice, she thought, though she couldn't hear the words, sounded very excited.

A few moments later she heard her own name called.

"What is it?" she asked, leaning over the banister. From the hall below the Siamese grinned up at her like a Cheshire cat.

"Harm! Harm!" she cried. "You'll never believe this! That was Mummy's sister, Auntie Jessica, you know, the one who married an American—and she's my godmother too—and she was calling from California and they want me to fly over next Tuesday and stay for two whole weeks and they're going to pay all the fares and everything! Isn't it amazing? Anyone would think you were a magician!"

CHAPTER 8

Yield

For the next couple of days—it was a weekend—
everything in the Parker household was sweetness and
light.

Melody was delighted at the prospect of her trip.
Mrs. Parker was pleased because Melody was de-
lighted. And Mr. Parker was content because Mrs.
Parker was pleased.

As for Harmony, it was enjoyable to think that this
unusually sunny atmosphere had been brought about
by her.

"Or rather," as she said to her audience in the chicken
house, "by the power of the Queen's Nose."

She took the coin out of the pocket of the new, still
quite pink, jeans, and began to play the game of
changing the royal expression.

"Sometimes at school," she said to the royal profile,
"they call me Nosey Parker." The Queen looked dis-
approving.

"It's just a joke about my last name, you know.
I'm not particularly inquisitive. And I haven't really
got much of a nose." The Queen's expression softened
a little.

"As for your nose, why, it's 'Royal not Roman

straight not snub,' you know." The Queen grinned. "Question is—what shall I use it for next?"

Harmony was still asking herself this several days later. Melody had gone, in new clothes and a fever of excitement. They had found her a seat on a standby flight, and had stood together watching the big jumbo pull away from Heathrow Airport.

On the drive home Harmony sat in the back of the car without speaking. Her silence was misunderstood.

"You'll miss her, won't you, darling?" cooed the Pouter.

This produced a rapid series of faces by way of reply—the Here We Go Again followed by the I Hate My Sister and topped off with the My Mother Drives Me Mad.

The Sea Lion caught sight of this display in the rear-view mirror.

"Don't be so silly, Harmony," he barked.

Harmony ducked down behind the seat wearing

the Don't Be So Silly Harmony Face. She stayed down until she had changed to the No Torture On Earth Can Make Me Do What You Say, and finally to the Private Joke. Then she surfaced, expressionless.

"Your younger daughter," sighed the Sea Lion.

That evening Harmony was herding Anita around the orchard, Rex Ruff Monty swinging from her hand. She wore the Concentrated Thought Face. What with wasting one and using one on Melody, the Queen's Nose had only brought her three wishes. And only one of those was an animal. Not that she regretted the watch or the Icebreaker, they were ace. But when she'd had that first conversation with Uncle Ginger, when he'd said that he knew a bit about magic, that he might be able to help, it was really only animals she'd been wishing for, lots of animals, all sorts of different pets.

Now there were only two wishes left.

"Right," said Harmony to Rex Ruff Monty, "my mind's made up," and she invented a new face to fit that statement, eyes narrowed, lips pressed closely together, chin stuck out.

"You mustn't be hurt," she said. "There'll never be anyone quite like you. But I am going to wish for something I have always longed for. I am going to wish for a puppy. And not just any puppy. I know exactly what I want, and the Queen's Nose will get it for me."

She took out the coin and addressed the Queen.

83

"Now this is going to be difficult," she said very seriously, "because when I'm ready I'm going to ask for a black Labrador. I can't possibly afford to buy one, let alone pay for his food and vet's bills. I haven't even got enough money for a collar and leash, and I can't imagine where he'll come from, or how they will allow me to keep him. But I'm not worried about any of that because your nose will fix it, somehow. What does worry me is that it's getting on toward the end of the summer holidays. And that means I shall be back at school just at the most important time in this puppy's life, just when we should be spending as much time together as possible."

The Queen looked extremely serious.

"I wish I didn't have to . . ." began Harmony slowly.

"That's it!" cried Harmony loudly, wearing the Suddenly Realizing Face.

The Queen managed a small smile.

"That's it," (switching to the Ridiculously Happy), "I needn't! I needn't go back to school! That can be the sixth wish and the Labrador puppy can be the seventh! Then I'll have all the time till Christmas to play with him and exercise him and start his training and everything!"

The last face she adopted was of course the My Mind's Made Up.

"That's what I'll do," said Harmony, and, just for an instant, the Queen looked very sad.

When a full-fed Anita had been persuaded back into

the chicken house, Harmony shut her in for the night as usual. The door was held closed by a latch.

Maybe because her mind was so full of her newly decided plans for the sixth and seventh wishes, she did not turn it carefully enough, so that it was only just holding the door shut. Perhaps Anita may have bumped against it from the inside. But only Rex Ruff Monty, looking back with his one glass eye as they went away up the orchard, saw the chicken house door swing gently open again and a spotty shape hop out and lope away among the twilit trees.

Harmony did not use the Queen's Nose that night. She had often heard the Sea Lion speak of "sleeping on" a decision, so she slept on this one. But she woke convinced it was right. She could not for the life of her see how she could suddenly have a term off school or how it could be decided now when there were still more than two weeks of the holidays to go. But she trusted absolutely in the power, and had no doubt it could be arranged, somehow.

She dressed, and took out the fifty pence piece.

Carefully, taking her time, she put her finger upon that magic edge, and rubbed for the sixth time.

"I *wish*," said Harmony, "that I won't be able to go to school this term."

She put the coin back in her pocket, picked up Rex Ruff Monty by his soft leg, and went downstairs.

At first, when she found the chicken house open and empty, Harmony was not particularly worried. Anita, she felt sure, would not have gone far. But when she had searched the orchard, and then the lawn and the flower beds and the vegetable patch and the shrubbery, and found no sign of her, she remembered the Newt's words with a kind of horror. "I saw this rabbit out in the road," he had said.

She ran out through the front gate but the road was empty in the early morning. She dashed for the Icebreaker, stuffed Rex Ruff Monty into the saddlebag, and wheeled the bike out onto the pavement.

Which way should she go?

At that moment she heard a distant whistling and saw in the distance the Canary hopping out of his little cage.

"Oh, please," cried Harmony when she reached him, "have you seen my rabbit? She's white with black spots. She's escaped."

The Canary looked at the face upturned to his. It was in fact the Pleading Face, but for once it was a natural expression. Harmony was much too upset to act. He shook his yellow head.

"Sorry, my love," chirped the Canary, "she hasn't come this way."

Quickly Harmony turned the Icebreaker and pedaled away, back past her own front door and off in the other direction. Before long she met the Kangaroo, pulling a packet of letters from his pouch, but he too shook his long sheeplike head.

By now Harmony was frantic with worry. It was beginning to dawn upon her that Anita could have been at liberty for a long time, perhaps all night. Suppose she had gone as far as the main road! She urged the Icebreaker to its greatest speed, the hum of already busy traffic reaching her ears, her mind in a whirl of anxiety, her eyes darting from side to side as she searched for a spotted shape in every front garden that she passed.

She did not see the sign that said "YIELD," and she did not hear the car that hit her.

CHAPTER 9

Good News, Bad News

It was some time since the accident. Immediately after it, had she been conscious, Harmony would surely have felt that the magic of the Queen's Nose was black, the work of an evil power.

Anita was lost, the Icebreaker a twisted wreck, and she herself flung in the gutter like a crumpled doll, the digital watch smashed on her broken wrist. And as well as the wrist, the hospital had had to deal with a fractured thigh, and some busted ribs and a collarbone, not to mention enough cuts and bruises to last a lifetime.

At first everything had seemed like one unending dream of strange voices and strange smells and pain. Sometimes the dream was not so bad, just a hazy muddle of spotted rabbits and shining black puppies; and sometimes it was a nightmare, always the same one. Rolling down a long road toward her came a giant fifty pence piece, a monstrous wheel as high as a house, that bore down upon her with a horrid clicking sound as it turned from one of its seven huge edges to the next. And she could not move, and she knew that the edge that would crush her would be the one at which the enormous Queen's enormous nose pointed. And she would cry out in terror.

The first afternoon that Harmony was really back in the world again, when she had fully understood what had happened and where she was, and was becoming used to all the strappings and plaster and the strange contraption that held her leg suspended, all the family was sitting around her bed.

Melody had cut short her holiday by a couple of days. Mr. Parker had taken time off from his office. Mrs. Parker had been beside her younger daughter all the while.

Harmony looked at them all in turn, and for once she did not see a vain Siamese Cat and a pompous Sea Lion and a fussy Pouter Pigeon. Instead she saw three worried people looking at her with love. She burst into tears.

Suddenly everything seemed all right.

"Don't worry, Harm. Your rabbit's quite OK. That funny little milkman with the squeaky voice found it, in the next door garden, and I'm looking after it, and it's fine."

"Don't worry, Harmony. We'll get you a new bike and a new watch."

"Don't worry, darling, I haven't thrown your jeans away this time, just washed them. And I went through the pockets. And that precious old fifty pence piece of yours is safe in your piggy bank."

When it was time to leave, Mrs. Parker stayed behind in the ward for a moment after the others had gone.

"Try and get a good rest tonight," she said. "Everything's going to be all right."

"I'm glad. I've been having awful dreams."

"I know. You've been shouting out."

"What did I shout?"

"It sounded like 'The Queen knows,' but I've no

idea what the Queen was supposed to know and I don't expect you have either."

"Mummy."

"Yes, darling?"

"What about school?"

"Oh, I'm afraid you won't be able to go to school this term."

The Queen knows all right, thought Harmony, she sure took care of the sixth wish. I bet if I could pick her out of the piggy bank she'd be grinning all over her face at the thought of a Labrador puppy let loose in here. The seventh wish is going to have to wait awhile.

Rex Ruff Monty seemed to enjoy being in the hospital. The saddlebag had been torn in the accident, but he had been quite unhurt. Mrs. Parker had brought him in, and he was waiting on top of the bedside locker when Harmony first came around. Now of course he was on the pillow beside her head, and the ward Sister (herself a Wire-haired Fox Terrier, Harmony had noted right away) had put beside the card over the bed saying "Harmony Parker" another which read "R. R. Monty." At snack time he was always given a sweet biscuit. It was never wasted.

At first, for someone who liked to be mostly by herself, it was worrying to be surrounded by so many people, patients and staff, from whom you could not escape. Harmony got over this by her usual method of turning people into animals.

As well as the Sister, there was a staff nurse with pop eyes and a very squashy sort of nose (Pug), a night nurse with very large spectacles who moved softly around the darkened ward, her uniform seeming to change color as she moved in and out of little pools of light (a Chameleon of course), and a pair of candy stripers who flitted about at high speed, chattering away nonstop at the patients and each other (Magpies).

There were two doctors whom she saw often. One she imagined was rather important, for the Wire-haired Fox Terrier and the Pug came rushing to his side whenever he appeared. But he didn't act importantly; he was quiet and small and sandy and quick, so he had to be a Ferret. The other one was younger, with red hair and a loud voice. He was a Howler Monkey.

And of course on either side of Harmony and all around the children's ward were a host of little animals who had damaged their wings or their hooves or their beaks from falling out of trees or into holes or running across roads without looking; so that she was able to fill a whole new sketching book with her own particular kind of drawings while she lay and mended.

At last the day came, when she had progressed from wheelchair to crutches to canes, on which the Ferret said that she might go home, and what a day that was.

There were fish sticks and baked beans and french

fries and catsup for lunch, as the Pouter Pigeon fussed over her.

The Siamese positively purred as she showed her how well and sleek and happy Anita was.

And in the evening, when the Sea Lion came back from doing his tricks in the city, he helped her out to the garage, and there was the Icebreaker, its dark blue paint shining, its chromium gleaming, its white-walled tires spotless.

"It looks as though it's never even been ridden," said Harmony slowly.

The Sea Lion barked with amusement.

"It hasn't," he said. "That's what comes of being a celebrity. When the manager of the bicycle shop heard that it was you who'd been involved in an accident and that the famous ten thousandth model had been smashed, he thought he'd help himself to another nice slice of publicity. He persuaded the manufacturers to give you a new Icebreaker. They'll be around to take your picture again any day now. You must be the only girl in the world who's ever been given two brand-new bicycles."

"I must be the only girl in the world who's ever been given a magic 1973 fifty pence piece," said Harmony to Rex Ruff Monty that night, as they lay in the familiar bed in the familiar room and watched the moon climb through the black branches of the apple trees. "And its power isn't done with yet. What's more, everyone's being so nice to me, even Simple

Sissie, that I'm really beginning to believe they might not object if I had a puppy."

As soon as she was home, she had transferred the coin from the pig's stomach to her pocket once more; and now she reached out of bed and took it out. She held the Queen's face up to the moonlight. It had looked very sad, she remembered, on the night before her accident. Now it wore a strange secret expression, not exactly crafty, more . . . Harmony searched her mind for the right word . . . more . . . knowing, that was it, knowing.

"I wonder," said Harmony to the Queen, "if you do know, already, what my seventh wish is going to be? I shouldn't be surprised. Anyway, if you don't, tomorrow you'll find out," and she put the coin away, settled Rex Ruff Monty, and went to sleep.

When she woke the next morning, a misty autumn morning with a chill in the air, she could not at first remember where she was and for an instant looked about for all the little animals in the children's ward. That led of course to the Suddenly Realizing Face quickly followed by the Ridiculously Happy.

She sat up in bed and looked out of the window. Down the road she could see the Kangaroo bounding along from house to house. Will he stop at ours, she thought? Not that it matters whether he does or not, because I'm at home and I'm feeling miles better and I'm going to use my seventh wish today and become the proud owner of a beautiful, sleek, shiny black Labrador puppy. So who cares whether the old Kangaroo has anything in his pouch for us. It's not important.

But he did have something, and it was.

When Harmony came down to breakfast, carefully, using only one cane now, she could see immediately that something was terribly wrong. The Sea Lion sat alone at the table—it was a Saturday, so he did not have to go and balance anything—holding a letter. His droopy mustache seemed to have drooped even lower and his eyes looked very sad.

"What is it?" said Harmony.

"It's about Ginger," said the Sea Lion, passing a flipper over his bald crown.

"About Uncle Ginger?" said Harmony in a small voice. "Why about him? Why couldn't he write himself?"

"He's ill."

"Very ill?"

"Very, very ill."

Over the past weeks Harmony's view of her family had changed. Maybe it was something to do with the accident or perhaps the Queen's Nose had a part in it. Maybe she was simply growing up. But she had only just realized that her father, for example, was not, as she had always thought, a person without much in the way of feelings but someone who found it difficult to show them.

She knew now what he felt for her. She could see, plainly, what he felt for his brother, very different kinds of people though they were. She put an arm around his shoulder.

"Daddy?"

"Mm."

"Is . . . Uncle Ginger going to die?"

For a couple of minutes Mr. Parker did not reply. With one hand he drummed on the typewritten letter in front of him. With the other he held Harmony's.

"This letter," he said at last, "is from the doctor who is treating him in a hospital in Bengal. Uncle Ginger has a horrible thing called Blackwater Fever. It doesn't sound from this that there's much hope for him."

"How shall we know, if . . . ?"

"They'll let us know by telegraph, they say."

Oh, Kangaroo, thought Harmony, how stupidly happy I was when I watched you this morning, not caring whether you came to our house. And now . . .

"Isn't there even the smallest chance that he'll get better, Daddy?"

The Sea Lion shook his head slowly. He picked up the letter and read from it. " '. . . I think it only right to tell you that in my opinion your brother may not have many days to live. His remarkable physical condition has kept him going thus far, but it is only fair to say that nothing short of a miracle can save him now.' "

He rose from the table and went heavily out of the room to tell the others.

Harmony's heart was thumping like a mad thing.

"Nothing short of a miracle!" She snatched up the envelope and peered at the postmark. A week ago. If she could only be in time!

She put her hand in her pocket.

CHAPTER 10

Christmas Present

Harmony was in such a frantic hurry to put the Queen's Nose to work that she did not stop for a moment to consider how she should word the wish. And as for the Labrador puppy, the thought of it never even crossed her mind. She simply yanked the coin out of her pocket, looked to make absolutely sure she had the right edge, rubbed, and spoke straight from her heart.

"I *wish* that Uncle Ginger will get better and come home and live near us and never go back to India again."

She looked quickly at the Queen's face, and the Queen smiled—there was no doubt about it. And somehow, strangely, the fifty pence piece felt different in her hand. Afterward she couldn't exactly think how. It looked the same; there were the nine clasped hands encircling its value and its date; there were D.G.Reg.F.D. and Elizabeth II; there was that familiar likeness of which she knew so well every fold of the dress, every wave of the hair, every cusp of the crown, and all the many expressions that flitted across the royal face. But the coin did feel different, lighter, almost pliable, as though all the power had gone out of it.

Which of course it has, thought Harmony. Seven wishes, all gone. But will this one work quickly enough? How long does it take a wish to get to India? Automatically she looked at her watch, her new watch just like the other, mock snakeskin strap and all. She thought back through the other wishes. All had been granted immediately, or within a very short time of using the Queen's Nose. What was happening? Oh, why was India so far away?

After breakfast the telephone rang. In spite of his bulk, the Sea Lion was the first to reach it. As he answered, his voice, Harmony could hear, was not quite steady. But it was only one of Melody's friends.

"We could hear by phone, couldn't we, Daddy?" asked Harmony. "You can call up from India, can't you?"

"Oh, yes. We could hear by phone or we could get a cable or we may have to wait for a letter. I think we must hope it'll be by letter. Bad news travels fast, they say."

"And no news is good news," said her mother.

"And patience is a virtue," said Melody, and they all managed some sort of a smile.

In fact they heard nothing for a week. Every time the phone rang someone picked it up as though it were a poisonous snake, but it was always harmless. Every morning Harmony, first up as usual, watched tensely for the Kangaroo, half hoping, half fearing that he would stop, and when he did, looking quickly at the stamps. But, apart from one which gave her a fright for a moment—it was an American one, on a letter from Auntie Jessica—they were all English. On them the face of the Queen was utterly expressionless.

It was not until the following Saturday that the virtue of patience was rewarded. For once Harmony had overslept, and she woke to see the Sea Lion coming into her room in his dressing-gown, a great smile on his big round face. He was holding not one, but two letters.

"Miracles do happen," he said.

Later, after breakfast, when they had all read and reread them, one from the hospital doctor in Bengal and, enclosed in it, one, unbelievably, from Uncle Ginger himself, Harmony took the letters down to the chicken house, sat on the tea chest and read them both all over again to Rex Ruff Monty and Anita.

The doctor's, dated the previous Saturday—a week after his first—was cautiously, surprisedly, hopeful of the chances of recovery of Mr. Henry Parker, who, in the early hours of that afternoon, had in the writer's words "turned the corner." It was full of "ifs" and "buts" and long words whose meaning Harmony did not understand, but it made one thing plain enough. Uncle Ginger was alive and going to stay alive! The enclosure was proof of that, even though it was just a couple of lines of laborious scrawl.

"Still around—just!" it said. "Very tired. Forgive scribble. Love to you all. Ginger. P.S. Funny thing. Fever went like magic."

"I should think it was magic," Mrs. Parker had said. "No one's ever supposed to recover from that fever."

And Mr. Parker had remarked on the odd chance that, allowing for the difference in time in the two countries, his brother's recovery must have started at just about the moment when they had received the first letter.

"It must be Harmony up to her tricks," said Melody, laughing.

"Whatever do you mean?"

"Well, she made me wish, you know, and I said I wish I could go to America, and look what happened."

"Imagine that!" said the Sea Lion with a grin. "We've got a magician in the family! What's your next trick going to be, Harmony? Going to produce another rabbit perhaps—out of my hat?" and they had all laughed.

"They'd never believe it if I told them," said Harmony as she folded up the letters and let Anita out to graze. "Even if I told them that Uncle Ginger's going to come home and live near us and never go back to India again, they'd just say, 'Well, anyone could have guessed something like that.' But that's all going to happen, Rex Ruff Monty, because it was all part of the seventh wish."

Two months went by, two months in which many
letters flew between Wimbledon and Bengal, and then
came the day when they were all once again at Heathrow Airport, watching a big Air India jet taxi to a
standstill. And out of it came a crowd of ordinary
men and women and children and one unmistakable
Silvertip Grizzly. There was much more silver than
there had been in the summer and more lines in the
brown face, and he was thin. But the old smile was
there as he greeted them all, and for Harmony once
again a very small private wink.

And when they were all comfortably at home,
drinking tea ("They grow it in India, you know,"
said the Silvertip, grinning), everything came out just
as the Queen's Nose had ordained.

"You're really better, Ginger old boy?"

"I'll say! You should have seen me a couple of months ago."

"How much leave have they given you, Ginger dear?"

"Permanent, you could say. They've invalided me out. They've been quite generous with the pension and so forth."

"What will you do, Uncle Ginger?"

"Get fit again first, Melody, is the answer to that, I think. Like this other ex-patient has been doing. You look much better than I'd expected, Harmony."

"Oh, I'm quite OK."

"Not back at school though?"

"Oh, well you see I'm not *that* OK. And anyway there's not much of the term left."

"Yes, quite," said the Silvertip. "Sorry, Melody, I haven't really answered your question. I think what I should like to do is to find a little cottage in the country—not too far from here, I hope—with roses around the door, and a good bit of garden, perhaps with a stream at the bottom of it. And grow most of my own food. And keep some chickens, and maybe a goat. And of course I'll have to find a job when I'm stronger again, part time perhaps, something out-doors, I'm handy at most things."

"Will you have a dog?" said Harmony.

"Oh, definitely," said Uncle Ginger. "You should have a dog here, you know," he said to them all.

"I don't really like dogs."

"How do you know, Melody. You've never tried."

"Dogs are messy, Ginger dear."

"Not if they're properly trained. Be very good company for you when you're on your own. Best possible insurance against burglars, you know."

"Not fair on the animal, old boy, is it? Different matter in the country, but in Wimbledon . . ."

"You've got a biggish garden. And the Common's very close."

"Ha. Hm. Well, I don't know about that. I think we'll drop the subject, if you don't mind."

"Just as you wish," said Uncle Ginger.

It was too dark that evening for Harmony to show Anita to the Silvertip, but next morning she was duly admired, as were the Icebreaker and the replacement wristwatch. Once again Harmony perched, and the Silvertip sat on the tea chest, and they watched the rabbit eating her breakfast.

"You got one animal then?"

"Yes."

"You kept very quiet yesterday during all that talk about a dog."

"Yes."

"That was going to be the last wish, wasn't it?"

"Yes."

"Seems a bit feeble for me just to say 'Thank you.' "

"Don't thank me, Uncle Ginger, thank the Queen's Nose."

"Still got it?"

"Oh, yes, of course," said Harmony. She pulled

the coin out and handed it over.

Uncle Ginger held it up to the light from the little wire netting window. Absently he rubbed the edge opposite the Queen's Nose without saying anything. After a moment he gave it back and said, "Funny the way things happen, isn't it?"

He got up and ducked out under the low door. "Come on. Let's go and have a look around at all the local real estate agents. The sort of cottage I want may take a bit of finding."

In fact it took a month and an awful lot of looking at cottages that were too large or too small or too fancy or too run-down.

But when they did succeed, Harmony was somehow not in the least surprised to find that it was not too far away and that there was a little stream running past the end of its good-sized garden. Around the door of course there was a climbing rose.

By Christmas Uncle Ginger was settled in, so well settled that he invited them all to Christmas dinner. And after it—it was a Parker family tradition to wait until then—they all exchanged presents, and Melody took pictures with the beautiful camera he had just given her.

"Isn't it smashing!" she said to Harmony. "What did Uncle Ginger give you?"

"Oh," said the Silvertip Grizzly. "I almost forgot," and he went out of the room, leaving the door open.

Harmony looked at the Sea Lion and the Pouter

Pigeon and the Siamese Cat, and they all had the same expression on their different faces, secretive, expectant, half-smiling.

And suddenly there was a bumbling, blundering, pattering, shuffling noise, and in through the door lollopped two fat, satiny, coal-black creatures, and behind them was the Grizzly, grinning.

"Oh, Uncle Ginger, *what* a surprise!" cried Melody in a very artificial voice. "You've got *two* Labrador puppies!"

"Only one of them's mine," said Uncle Ginger.

Harmony swallowed.

"Whose is the other?" she said.

"Yours."

CHAPTER II

"*Perhaps Someone Will*"

There seemed to be so much to do—looking after her puppy (including some very early training in not biting either Rex Ruff Monty or Anita), and trips out to Rose Cottage to visit Uncle Ginger and his—that the Christmas holidays were over and Harmony was back at school again before she ever really gave a thought to the fifty pence piece again.

All that time it had lain in the piggy bank, and one Sunday morning Harmony took it out and had a long look at that nose that had made so many changes in her life.

"What am I to do with you?" she said to the Queen. Uncle Ginger was coming to lunch; she would ask his advice.

That afternoon the two of them (everyone else said it was so cold) took the puppies up onto the Common. And as they walked and watched them running and playing, Harmony took the magic coin out of her pocket.

"What shall I do with it, Uncle Ginger?" she said. "Do I just keep it for always? Remember the instruc-

109

tions: 'Do not spend and do not lend, Change me not to please a friend.' "

"Oh, I think that only applied while the coin was working for you," said the Silvertip. "After all, you've had all seven wishes, so it doesn't matter now, does it? You might just as well use it. It'll still buy you fifty pence worth of something."

"Oh, I don't think I want to do that."

They walked further.

"Uncle Ginger?"

"Yes."

"D'you suppose that the Queen's Nose . . . could work . . . for someone else . . . if they had it?"

The Silvertip Grizzly stopped in his tracks and turned and looked at her.

"I suppose it might," he said slowly.

"After all," he said with a smile, "miracles do happen."

Harmony took one last look at the face of the Queen, and particularly at the silver tip of that nose.

Then she drew back her arm, and with all her strength she threw the piece of money far, far away into the thick wintery grasses of Wimbledon Common.

"Perhaps someone will be lucky," she said, and they walked on.

Perhaps someone will.

Siamese Cat.

Silvertip Grizzly.